THIS BOOK

BELONGS TO

::

::

Thank you for Purchasing my book and taking the time to read it from front to back. I am always grateful when a reader chooses my work and I hope you enjoyed it!

With the vast selection available online, I am touched that you chose to be purchasing my work and take valuable time out of your life to read it. My hope is that you feel you made the right decision.

I very much would like to know what you thought of the book. Please take the time to write an honest and informative review on Amazon.com. Your experience and opinions will be of great benefit to me and those readers looking to make an informed choice.

With much thanks.

Table of Contents

SUMMARY

Crochet tank tops have gained immense popularity in recent years due to their unique and alluring qualities. These tops are not only fashionable but also versatile, making them a must-have item in any fashion-conscious individual's wardrobe.

One of the main reasons why crochet tank tops are so appealing is their intricate and delicate design. The art of crochet involves creating fabric by interlocking loops of yarn using a crochet hook. This technique allows for the creation of beautiful and intricate patterns, resulting in a visually stunning garment. The intricate details of crochet tank tops make them stand out from other types of tank tops, adding a touch of elegance and sophistication to any outfit.

Another reason why crochet tank tops are so alluring is their versatility. These tops can be styled in numerous ways, making them suitable for various occasions. They can be paired with high-waisted jeans or shorts for a casual and effortless look, or dressed up with a skirt and heels for a more formal event. The versatility of crochet tank tops allows individuals to express their personal style and experiment with different looks, making them a staple in any fashion enthusiast's wardrobe.

Furthermore, crochet tank tops are often handmade, adding to their appeal. Handmade items are highly valued in today's fast-paced and mass-produced world, as they are seen as unique and one-of-a-kind. The craftsmanship and attention to detail that goes into creating a crochet tank top make it a special and cherished piece of clothing. Additionally, the handmade nature of these tops often means that they are made with high-quality materials, ensuring durability and longevity.

In addition to their aesthetic appeal, crochet tank tops also offer practical benefits. The open and breathable nature of crochet fabric makes these tops perfect for warm weather. They allow for air circulation, keeping the wearer cool and comfortable even on the hottest of days. This makes crochet tank tops a go-to choice for summer outings, beach trips, or any occasion where comfort is a priority.

Overall, the allure of crochet tank tops lies in their intricate design, versatility, handmade craftsmanship, and practicality. These tops not only make a fashion statement but also offer a unique and individualistic touch to any outfit. Whether you're looking to add a touch of elegance to your casual attire or make a statement at a special event, crochet tank tops are the perfect choice."

In recent years, there has been a growing need for innovation in warmer weather crochet fashion. Crochet, a traditional craft that involves creating fabric by interlocking loops of yarn with a crochet hook, has long been associated with cozy and winter-appropriate garments such as sweaters, scarves, and hats. However, as fashion trends evolve and consumers seek more versatile and seasonally appropriate options, there is a demand for crochet designs that are suitable for warmer weather.

One of the main challenges in adapting crochet fashion for warmer climates is the choice of materials. Traditional crochet yarns, which are often made of wool or other heavy fibers, can be too warm and uncomfortable to wear in hot weather. Therefore, designers and manufacturers need to explore alternative materials that are lightweight, breathable, and moisture-wicking. This could include using cotton or linen yarns, which are known for their ability to keep the body cool and dry.

Another aspect that requires innovation in warmer weather crochet fashion is the design itself. Traditional crochet patterns often feature dense and intricate stitches, which can create a heavy and bulky fabric. To make crochet garments more suitable for warmer weather, designers need to experiment with openwork stitches and lace-like patterns that allow for better air circulation. This not only enhances the breathability of the fabric but also adds a touch of elegance and femininity to the designs.

Furthermore, the silhouette and style of crochet garments need to be reimagined for warmer weather. While winter crochet fashion often focuses on oversized and cozy pieces, warmer weather crochet fashion calls for lighter and more fitted designs. This could include cropped tops, lightweight cardigans, and breezy dresses that showcase the beauty of crochet while keeping the wearer comfortable in higher temperatures.

In addition to adapting the materials, design, and silhouette, innovation in warmer weather crochet fashion also involves incorporating modern elements and trends. This could mean incorporating vibrant colors, playful patterns, or even incorporating other materials such as beads or sequins to add a touch of glamour to the crochet pieces. By combining traditional crochet techniques with contemporary aesthetics, designers can create crochet fashion that appeals to a wider audience and meets the demands of the modern fashion industry.

Overall, the need for innovation in warmer weather crochet fashion is evident. As consumers seek crochet garments that are suitable for all seasons, designers and manufacturers must rise to the challenge and explore new materials, designs, and styles. By doing so, they can not only meet the demands of the market but also showcase the versatility and beauty of crochet as a fashion"

"A. Tools and materials for crochet include a variety of items that are essential for this craft. Firstly, you will need crochet hooks, which come in different sizes and are used to create the loops and stitches in your crochet work. These hooks can be made from various materials such as aluminum, plastic, or bamboo, each offering a different feel and grip.

In addition to crochet hooks, you will also need yarn. Yarn comes in a wide range of colors, textures, and thicknesses, allowing you to create different effects and designs in your crochet projects. It is important to choose the right yarn for your project, considering factors such as the desired drape, warmth, and durability.

To keep track of your progress and count stitches, it is helpful to have stitch markers and a tape measure. Stitch markers are small, removable markers that can be placed on your work to indicate specific stitches or sections. They are particularly useful when working on complex patterns or when shaping your crochet piece. A tape measure is essential for ensuring that your finished project meets the desired dimensions.

Another important tool for crochet is a yarn needle or tapestry needle. This needle has a large eye and a blunt tip, making it easy to thread yarn through and weave in loose ends. It is used to finish off your crochet work neatly and securely.

To enhance your crochet projects, you may also want to consider using additional tools and materials. These can include crochet stitch guides or pattern books, which provide instructions and inspiration for different stitches and designs. Blocking mats and pins are useful for shaping and stretching your finished crochet pieces, ensuring that they lay flat and have a professional finish.

Overall, having the right tools and materials for crochet is essential for a successful and enjoyable crafting experience. By investing in quality hooks, yarn, and other accessories, you can create beautiful and intricate crochet projects that showcase your creativity and skill."

Basic crochet stitches and techniques are the foundation of any crochet project. These stitches are the building blocks that allow you to create a wide variety of patterns and designs. Whether you are a beginner or an experienced crocheter, it is essential to have a solid understanding of these basic stitches in order to successfully complete any crochet project.

One of the most commonly used basic crochet stitches is the chain stitch. This stitch is the starting point for almost every crochet project and is used to create the foundation row. The chain stitch is created by making a loop with the yarn and pulling it through the loop on the hook. This process is repeated until the desired number of chains is achieved.

Once the foundation row is complete, the next basic stitch to learn is the single crochet stitch. This stitch is used to create a tight and dense fabric. To make a single crochet stitch, you insert the hook into the next stitch, yarn over, and pull the yarn through the stitch. Then, yarn over again and pull through both loops on the hook. This completes one single crochet stitch.

Another important basic stitch is the double crochet stitch. This stitch is taller than the single crochet stitch and creates a looser and more open fabric. To make a double crochet stitch, you yarn over, insert the hook into the next stitch, yarn over again, and pull the yarn through the stitch. Then, yarn over once more and pull through the first two loops on the hook. Yarn over again and pull through the remaining two loops on the hook to complete the double crochet stitch.

In addition to these basic stitches, there are several other techniques that are commonly used in crochet. One such technique is increasing, which is used to add stitches and create a wider fabric. This is typically done by working multiple stitches into the same stitch or by working stitches into the gaps between stitches.

Decreasing is another important technique that is used to remove stitches and create shaping in a crochet project. This is typically done by working two stitches together or by skipping stitches in a row.

Other techniques include changing colors, which allows you to create intricate patterns and designs, and working in the round, which is used to create circular or tubular projects such as hats or amigurumi.

Overall, mastering basic crochet stitches and techniques is essential for any crocheter. These stitches provide the foundation for all crochet projects and allow you to create a wide variety of patterns and designs. Whether you are a beginner or an experienced crocheter, it is"

When it comes to considering body shape and style preferences, there are several factors to take into account in order to achieve the desired outcome. Body shape plays a crucial role in determining what styles and cuts will flatter an individual's figure, while style preferences reflect personal taste and fashion choices.

Firstly, understanding one's body shape is essential in selecting clothing that enhances their best features and minimizes any areas they may feel less confident about. There are generally five main body shapes: hourglass, pear, apple, rectangle, and inverted triangle. Each shape has its own unique characteristics and requires different styling techniques.

For instance, individuals with an hourglass figure have well-defined waists and balanced proportions between their bust and hips. They can opt for fitted clothing that accentuates their curves, such as wrap dresses or high-waisted bottoms. On the other hand, those with a pear-shaped body have narrower shoulders and wider hips. They can choose A-line skirts or dresses that draw attention to their upper body and create a more balanced silhouette.

Additionally, considering style preferences is crucial in creating a wardrobe that reflects one's personality and individuality. Style preferences can vary greatly from person to person, ranging from classic and elegant to edgy and trendy. Some individuals may prefer a more minimalistic approach, while others may enjoy experimenting with bold prints and colors.

Taking into account both body shape and style preferences, it is important to strike a balance between what is flattering and what makes the individual feel confident and comfortable. This can be achieved by understanding the principles of proportion, color theory, and garment construction.

Proportion is key in creating a visually pleasing outfit. For example, pairing a loose-fitting top with fitted bottoms can create a balanced look for those with a rectangle body shape. Color theory can also be utilized to highlight certain areas or create illusions. Darker colors tend to have a slimming effect, while lighter colors can draw attention to specific areas.

Lastly, understanding garment construction is essential in selecting pieces that fit well and flatter the body shape. Paying attention to details such as fabric, cut, and tailoring can make a significant difference in how clothing drapes and fits on the body.

In conclusion, considering body shape and style preferences is crucial in creating a wardrobe that not only flatters an individual's figure but also reflects their personal taste and fashion choices. By understanding one's body shape, selecting appropriate styles, and paying attention to proportion, color theory, and garment construction, one can confidently"

"When it comes to designing for different skill levels, it is important to consider the abilities and experience of the target audience. Adapting designs to cater to different skill levels can greatly enhance the user experience and ensure that individuals of varying proficiency levels can engage with the product or service effectively.

One key aspect to consider when adapting designs is the complexity of the user interface. For beginners or individuals with limited technical skills, it is crucial to simplify the interface and make it intuitive and easy to navigate. This can be achieved by using clear and concise labels, providing visual cues, and minimizing the number of steps required to complete a task. By reducing the cognitive load and eliminating unnecessary complexities, beginners can quickly grasp the functionality of the design and feel more confident in using it.

On the other hand, for more advanced users or individuals with higher skill levels, it is important to provide additional features and functionalities that cater to their expertise. This can include advanced settings, customization options, and shortcuts that allow them to streamline their workflow and perform tasks more efficiently. By offering these advanced features, experienced users can fully utilize their skills and maximize their productivity.

Another aspect to consider when adapting designs for different skill levels is the availability of help and support. Beginners may require more guidance and assistance, so providing clear instructions, tooltips, and tutorials can greatly enhance their learning experience. Advanced users, on the other hand, may prefer access to comprehensive documentation, forums, or even direct support from experts. By offering different levels of support, designers can ensure that users of all skill levels can easily access the information they need to effectively use the product or service.

Furthermore, it is important to conduct user testing and gather feedback from individuals of different skill levels during the design process. This can help identify any usability issues or areas where improvements can be made to better accommodate the needs of different users. By involving users in the design process, designers can gain valuable insights and make informed decisions to create a more inclusive and user-friendly experience.

In conclusion, adapting designs for different skill levels is crucial to ensure that individuals of varying proficiency levels can effectively engage with a product or service. By simplifying the interface for beginners and providing advanced features for experienced users, designers can create a more inclusive and user-friendly experience. Additionally, offering appropriate levels of help and support, as well as involving users in the design process, can further enhance the usability and effectiveness of the design."

To create a timeless tank top, you will need the following materials: fabric (preferably a lightweight and breathable material such as cotton or linen), a sewing machine, thread, scissors, pins, measuring tape, and a tank top pattern (which can be purchased or created by tracing an existing tank top).

1. Start by selecting your fabric. Consider the desired color, pattern, and texture of your tank top. It's important to choose a fabric that is comfortable to wear and suitable for the season.

2. Take your measurements using a measuring tape. Measure your bust, waist, and hips, as well as the desired length of your tank top. These measurements will help you determine the appropriate size of the tank top pattern.

3. Once you have your measurements, find or create a tank top pattern that matches your size. If you're using a purchased pattern, follow the instructions provided to cut out the appropriate size. If you're creating your own pattern, lay your existing tank top on a large piece of paper and trace around it, adding seam allowances as necessary.

4. Lay your fabric flat on a clean, spacious surface. Place the tank top pattern on top of the fabric, aligning the grainline (indicated on the pattern) with the grain of the fabric. Pin the pattern to the fabric to secure it in place.

5. Carefully cut out the fabric following the outline of the pattern. Take your time to ensure accurate and clean cuts. Remove the pins and set aside the pattern for later use.

6. With the fabric pieces cut out, it's time to start sewing. Begin by sewing the shoulder seams together. Place the right sides of the fabric together and pin them in place. Using a sewing machine, stitch along the pinned edges, securing the shoulder seams. Remember to backstitch at the beginning and end of each seam to reinforce the stitches.

7. Next, sew the side seams of the tank top. Again, place the right sides of the fabric together and pin them in place. Stitch along the pinned edges, starting from the bottom hem and ending at the armhole. Backstitch at the beginning and end of each seam.

8. Now it's time to finish the neckline and armholes. Fold the raw edges of the fabric towards the inside of the tank top, creating a clean edge. Pin the folded edges in place and stitch along them, creating a neat finish. You can use a straight stitch or a zigzag stitch,"

To create a bohemian-inspired crochet tank top, you will need a few essential materials and a basic understanding of crochet techniques. This project is perfect for those who love the boho style and want to add a unique and handmade piece to their wardrobe.

First, gather your materials. You will need a crochet hook, preferably in a size suitable for the yarn you choose. Speaking of yarn, opt for a lightweight and breathable material, such as cotton or bamboo, to ensure comfort when wearing the tank top. Additionally, consider selecting yarn in earthy tones or vibrant colors commonly associated with bohemian fashion.

Next, familiarize yourself with the basic crochet stitches. The tank top will typically involve using single crochet, double crochet, and chain stitches. If you are new to crochet, there are numerous online tutorials and instructional books available to help you learn these stitches.

Once you have your materials and basic crochet knowledge, it's time to start creating your tank top. Begin by crocheting a foundation chain that matches the desired width of the tank top. This chain will serve as the base for the first row of stitches.

After completing the foundation chain, work your way up by crocheting rows of stitches. The specific pattern and stitch combinations will depend on the design you have in mind. For a bohemian-inspired tank top, you might consider incorporating lace-like stitches, intricate patterns, or even fringe details.

As you progress, make sure to periodically try on the tank top to ensure it fits well and adjust the size if necessary. Remember that crochet fabric can stretch, so it's essential to account for this when determining the final measurements.

Once you have completed the main body of the tank top, it's time to add any desired embellishments. Bohemian fashion often includes decorative elements such as tassels, beads, or embroidery. You can incorporate these details by attaching them to the tank top using a crochet hook or sewing them on afterward.

Finally, finish off your crochet tank top by adding straps. You can create simple shoulder straps using chains or opt for more intricate designs, such as braided or macramé straps. Experiment with different styles to find the one that best complements your overall bohemian aesthetic.

Once your tank top is complete, give it a gentle wash and block it to ensure the stitches settle into place and the fabric retains its shape. Then, proudly wear your bohemian-inspired crochet tank top and enjoy the compliments you'll receive on your unique"

Crafting a sporty crochet tank top is a fun and creative project that allows you to showcase your crochet skills while also adding a stylish and trendy piece to your wardrobe. Whether you're an experienced crocheter or a beginner looking to expand your skills, this project is suitable for all levels.

To start, you'll need to gather the necessary materials. This includes a crochet hook, preferably in a size suitable for the yarn you'll be using, and a sport-weight or lightweight yarn in the color of your choice. You may also want to have a tape measure, stitch markers, and a yarn needle on hand.

Once you have your materials ready, it's time to choose a pattern or design for your tank top. There are numerous patterns available online or in crochet books that cater specifically to sporty tank tops. You can opt for a simple and basic design or go for something more intricate with unique stitch patterns and details.

Before you begin crocheting, it's important to take accurate measurements of your bust, waist, and hips to ensure a proper fit. This will help you determine the size and shape of the tank top you'll be creating. You can refer to the pattern you've chosen for guidance on sizing and adjustments.

Next, you'll start crocheting the tank top by creating a foundation chain. This chain will serve as the base for the body of the tank top. You'll then work rows or rounds of stitches, following the pattern instructions, to create the desired length and width of the tank top.

As you progress, you may need to shape the tank top by increasing or decreasing stitches at certain points. This will help create a flattering fit and ensure that the tank top hugs your body in all the right places. The pattern you're following will provide guidance on when and how to make these adjustments.

Once you've completed the body of the tank top, it's time to move on to the straps. The straps can be made using the same stitch pattern as the body or you can opt for a different stitch pattern to add visual interest. You'll attach the straps to the front and back of the tank top, making sure they're evenly spaced and securely attached.

Finally, you'll finish off your crochet tank top by weaving in any loose ends and blocking the finished piece. Blocking involves wetting or steaming the tank top to help it relax and take its final shape. This step is crucial for achieving a professional and polished look.

Once your tank top is dry"

Crafting an intricate lace tank top requires a combination of skill, patience, and attention to detail. This delicate and elegant garment is a labor of love, as it involves working with fine threads and intricate patterns to create a stunning piece of wearable art.

To begin the process, one must carefully select the appropriate lace pattern. There are countless options available, ranging from simple and classic designs to more complex and ornate motifs. The chosen pattern will dictate the overall look and feel of the tank top, so it is crucial to choose one that aligns with the desired aesthetic.

Once the pattern is selected, the next step is to gather the necessary materials. High-quality lace thread, preferably in a color that complements the desired final product, is essential. Additionally, a set of fine knitting needles or crochet hooks, depending on the preferred technique, will be required. These tools must be chosen with care, as they need to be suitable for working with delicate lace threads.

With the pattern and materials in hand, the crafting process can begin. This involves carefully following the lace pattern, stitch by stitch, row by row. Each intricate detail must be meticulously executed to ensure the final result is flawless. This requires a steady hand and a keen eye for detail, as even the slightest mistake can disrupt the overall pattern and compromise the integrity of the tank top.

As the lace tank top takes shape, it is important to periodically check for any errors or inconsistencies. This can be done by laying the work flat and examining it closely, or by holding it up against the body to assess the fit and drape. Any mistakes or imperfections should be corrected promptly to maintain the high standard of craftsmanship.

The final stages of crafting an intricate lace tank top involve blocking and finishing. Blocking is the process of shaping the garment to its desired dimensions and allowing the lace to open up fully. This is typically done by pinning the tank top to a foam board or blocking mat and gently stretching it to the desired shape. Once blocked, the tank top is left to dry, allowing the lace to set and maintain its shape.

Finishing touches, such as adding straps or a decorative border, can be added to enhance the overall design. These details require careful consideration and should be in harmony with the lace pattern and the desired aesthetic of the tank top.

Crafting an intricate lace tank top is a time-consuming and intricate process that demands both technical skill and artistic vision. The end result, however, is a stunning and unique garment that"

"Vintage crochet tank tops have made a comeback in recent years, and it's no wonder why. These timeless pieces exude a sense of nostalgia and femininity that is hard to resist. Whether you're a fan of the bohemian look or simply appreciate the craftsmanship of yesteryear, revisiting vintage crochet tank top styles is a delightful way to add a touch of vintage charm to your wardrobe.

One of the most appealing aspects of vintage crochet tank tops is their versatility. They can be dressed up or down, making them suitable for a variety of occasions. Pair a delicate lace crochet tank top with a flowing maxi skirt and sandals for a romantic boho-inspired look perfect for a summer music festival. Alternatively, layer a chunky crochet tank top over a basic tee and jeans for a cozy and casual outfit that still exudes vintage flair.

The intricate crochet patterns and delicate details of vintage tank tops are a testament to the skill and artistry of the past. Each stitch is carefully crafted by hand, resulting in a unique and one-of-a-kind garment. The craftsmanship of vintage crochet tank tops is truly a work of art, and wearing one allows you to appreciate the time and effort that went into creating it.

In addition to their aesthetic appeal, vintage crochet tank tops also offer a sustainable fashion choice. By choosing to wear vintage or second-hand clothing, you are reducing your carbon footprint and supporting a more sustainable fashion industry. Vintage crochet tank tops are not only stylish but also eco-friendly, making them a win-win choice for fashion-conscious individuals.

When it comes to styling vintage crochet tank tops, the options are endless. They can be paired with high-waisted shorts for a retro-inspired look, or layered under a blazer for a more sophisticated ensemble. The key is to experiment and have fun with your outfit choices, allowing your vintage crochet tank top to be the focal point of your look.

In conclusion, revisiting vintage crochet tank top styles is a wonderful way to embrace the beauty and craftsmanship of the past. These timeless pieces offer versatility, sustainability, and a touch of vintage charm to any outfit. So why not add a vintage crochet tank top to your wardrobe and let its intricate details and unique design make a statement?"

"As the warmer weather approaches, it's time to start thinking about how to embrace it with style. Whether you're heading to the beach, attending outdoor events, or simply enjoying the sunshine, there are plenty of ways to make a fashion statement while staying comfortable.

One of the key elements of embracing warmer weather with style is choosing the right fabrics. Opt for lightweight and breathable materials such as cotton, linen, or silk. These fabrics allow air to circulate and prevent you from feeling overheated. Additionally, they have a natural ability to wick away moisture, keeping you cool and dry throughout the day.

When it comes to colors, embrace the vibrant and lively hues that are synonymous with summer. Think bright yellows, oranges, pinks, and blues. These colors not only reflect the sunny and cheerful atmosphere but also make a bold fashion statement. Don't be afraid to experiment with different color combinations and patterns to create a unique and eye-catching look.

Another important aspect of embracing warmer weather with style is choosing the right footwear. Swap out your heavy winter boots for lighter options such as sandals, espadrilles, or canvas sneakers. Not only will these shoes keep your feet cool, but they also add a touch of casual elegance to your outfit. Opt for neutral tones or playful prints to complement your summer wardrobe.

Accessories play a crucial role in completing your summer look. A wide-brimmed hat not only protects you from the sun but also adds a touch of sophistication to your outfit. Sunglasses are a must-have accessory to shield your eyes from the bright sunlight while adding a cool and trendy vibe. Don't forget to accessorize with statement jewelry, such as colorful beaded bracelets or layered necklaces, to add a touch of personality to your ensemble.

Lastly, don't forget to take care of your skin and hair during the warmer months. Use lightweight and oil-free moisturizers with SPF to protect your skin from harmful UV rays. Opt for hairstyles that keep your hair off your face and neck, such as braids, ponytails, or top knots, to stay cool and stylish.

In conclusion, embracing warmer weather with style is all about choosing the right fabrics, colors, footwear, accessories, and taking care of your skin and hair. By following these tips, you can create a fashionable and comfortable summer wardrobe that allows you to fully enjoy the sunny days ahead. So, embrace the warmth, step out in style, and make a statement wherever you go!"

While you are making the piece, it will look too big and too long. Don't worry—if your "after blocking" gauge matches the gauge specified in the pattern, your piece will shrink to the correct size when you wash it.

Gauge

Gauge is listed for each design in this book. This is simply a statement of how many stitches and how many rows are needed to make a 4"/10 cm square using the yarn and stitch pattern specified. If you do not match this gauge, your tank will not turn out the size you planned.

To test your gauge, begin by making a swatch at least 5"/12.7 cm square in the pattern stitch indicated. Block your swatch by washing and drying it the way you intend to wash and dry the finished garment. Then measure off a 4"/10 cm square in the center of your swatch and count the stitches and rows. If you have more stitches in 4"/10 cm than the pattern specifies, use a larger hook. If you have fewer stitches in 4"/10 cm than are called for, use a smaller hook. Adjust your hook size until you can match the gauge specification.

Fit

The bust measurement listed for each pattern is the actual finished garment measurement. These tanks and tunics are intended to comfortably skim the body, with a fit that is neither skintight nor oversized. To achieve this fit, choose the size closest to, but not smaller than, your actual bust measurement. If you are making one of the longer tunic designs, base your size choice on the larger of your bust or hip measurement.

Abbreviations

ch	chain
dc	double crochet

dc2tog	double crochet 2 together
dec	decrease (d)
hdc	half double crochet
hdc2tog	half double crochet 2 together
inc	increase (d)
patt	pattern
rem	remain (s) (ing)
rep	repeat
rnd(s)	round(s)
RS	right side
sc	single crochet
sc2tog	single crochet 2 together
sk	skip
sl st	slip stitch
sp(s)	space(s)
st(s)	stitch(es)
WS	wrong side

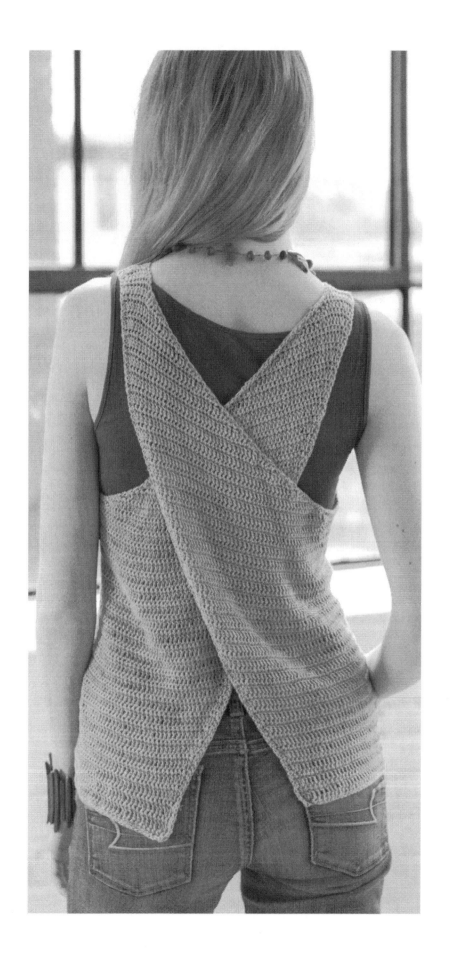

SKILL LEVEL
Intermediate

SIZES
Women's Extra Small (Small, Medium, Large, Extra Large)

FINISHED MEASUREMENTS
Bust: 30½ (34¼, 38, 42, 45¾)"/77.5 (87, 96.5, 106.5, 116) cm

YARN
Quince & Co. Sparrow, fine weight #2 yarn (100% organic linen; 168 yd./1.75 oz., 155 m/50 g per skein)
- 4 (5, 6, 6, 7) skeins #205 Little Fern

HOOKS & NOTIONS
- US size F-5/3.75 mm crochet hook
- Tapestry needle

GAUGE
21 sts and 13 rows in Alternating Rows patt = 4"/10 cm

PATTERN NOTE
- Octavia is worked in one piece from the bottom up. The only seams are at the shoulders.

STITCH PATTERN

Alternating Rows Pattern
Row 1 (RS): Ch3, sk first sc, dc in each sc to end, ending with dc in beginning ch-1.
Row 2 (WS): Ch1, sk first dc, sc in each dc to end, ending with sc in 3rd ch of beginning ch-3.
Rep Rows 1–2 for patt.

Body

Ch 147 (167, 187, 207, 227).

Row 1 (RS): Sc in 2nd ch from hook and in each ch to end, turn. 146 (166, 186, 206, 226) sc.

Row 2 (WS): Ch3, dc2 in first sc, dc in each sc to last 2 sc, dc2 in next sc, dc in next sc, turn. 2 sts inc.

Row 3: Ch1, sc in each dc to end, turn.

Rep [Rows 2–3] 21 (21, 22, 22, 23) more times. 190 (210, 232, 252, 274) sts.

Left Back

Row 1 (RS): Ch3, dc2 in first sc, dc in next 42 (46, 52, 55, 60) sc, dc2tog, hdc, sc, sl st, turn.

Row 2 (WS): Ch1, sl st in first 4 sts, ch1, sc in each dc to end. *Row 3:* Ch3, dc2 in first sc, dc in each sc to last 5 sc, dc2tog, hdc, sc, sl st, turn.

Row 4: Ch1, sl st in first 4 sts, ch1, sc in each dc to end.

Rep [Rows 3–4] 8 (9, 10, 11, 12) more times. 8 (8, 10, 9, 10) sts rem.

Work 4 (2, 0, 0, 0) rows even in Alternating Rows patt. Fasten off.

Front

With RS facing, sk 14 (16, 16, 20, 22) sts for armhole and rejoin yarn.

Row 1 (RS): Ch3, dc2tog, dc in next 60 (68, 78, 84, 92) sc, dc2tog, dc, turn.

Row 2 (WS): Ch1, sc2tog, sc in each dc to last 3 dc, sc2tog, sc, turn.

Row 3: Ch3, dc2tog, dc in each sc to last 3 sc, dc2tog, dc, turn.

Rep [Rows 2–3] 2 (4, 5, 5, 6) more times. 52 (52, 58, 64, 68) sts.

Work 13 (9, 7, 9, 9) rows even in Alternating Rows patt.

Shape Front Neck

Row 1 (RS): Ch3, dc 7 (7, 9, 8, 9), dc2tog, dc, turn.

Row 2 (WS): Ch1, sc2tog, sc in each dc to end. 8 (8, 10, 9, 10) sts rem.

Work 2 rows even in Alternating Rows patt.

Fasten off.

Sk 32 (32, 34, 42, 44) sts for center front neck and rejoin yarn.

Row 1 (RS): Ch3, dc2tog, dc in each sc to end, turn.

Row 2 (WS): Ch1, sc in each dc to last 3 sc, sc2tog, sc. 8 (8, 10, 9, 10) sts rem.

Work 2 rows even in Alternating Rows patt.

Fasten off.

With RS facing, sk 14 (16, 16, 20, 22) sts for armhole and rejoin yarn.

Row 1 (RS): Ch1, sl st, hdc, dc2tog, dc in each sc to last 2 sc, dc2 in next st, dc in last dc, turn.

Row 2 (WS): Ch1, sc in each st to last dc, sl st in top of dc2tog, turn.

Rep [Rows 1–2] 9 (10, 11, 12, 13) more times. 8 (8, 10, 9, 10) sts rem.

Work 4 (2, 0, 0, 0) rows even in Alternating Rows patt.

Fasten off.

Finishing

Sew shoulder seams, crossing right back over left back.

Edging

Join yarn at any shoulder seam. Work 1 rnd sc around edge. Surprisingly, there is only one edge on this piece, which winds around the armholes, neck, and lower edge.

Weave in ends. Block.

Sansome

With its deep, buttoned-front opening, this tunic is a sleek and versatile layering piece. The open stitch pattern creates a modern craft feeling.

SKILL LEVEL
Easy

SIZES
Women's Extra Small (Small, Medium, Large, Extra Large)

FINISHED MEASUREMENTS
Bust: 32¾ (36¼, 40, 43½, 47¼)"/83 (92, 101.5, 110.5, 120) cm

YARN
Kollage Yarns Riveting Sport, light weight #3 yarn (95% cotton, 5% other; 350 yd./3.5 oz., 320 m/100 g per skein)
- 3 (3, 3, 4, 4) skeins #7906 Cloud Denim

HOOKS & NOTIONS
- US size G-6/4.25 mm crochet hook
- Tapestry needle
- 8 buttons ½"/13 mm diameter
- Stitch marker

GAUGE
22 sts and 11 rows in Double Crochet Grid patt = 4"/10 cm

PATTERN NOTE
- Turning chain is not included in stitch counts.

STITCH PATTERN

Double Crochet Grid Pattern

Row 1 (WS): Ch1, sc in first dc, *ch4, sk 4 dc, sc in next dc; rep from * to end.

Row 2 (RS): Ch3, *dc4 in ch-4 sp, ch1; rep from * to end, ending with dc4 in ch-4 sp, dc in last sc.

Row 3: Ch1, sc in first dc, *ch4, sc in ch-1 sp; rep from * to end, ending with sc in 3rd ch of beginning ch-3.

Rep Rows 2–3 for patt.

Back

Ch 93 (103, 113, 123, 133).

Foundation row (WS): Dc in 4th ch from hook and in each ch to end. 90 (100, 110, 120, 130) dc.

Begin working Double Crochet Grid patt.

Work even in patt until piece measures 20"/51 cm, ending with a RS row.

Shape Armholes

Row 1 (WS): Ch1, sl st in each st to 2nd (2nd, 2nd, 3rd, 3rd) ch-1 sp, work in patt until 2 (2, 2, 3, 3) ch-1 sps remain, sc in 2nd (2nd, 2nd, 3rd, 3rd) ch-1 sp from end, turn.

Row 2 (Dec row) (RS): Ch3, dc2tog in ch-4 sp, dc2 in same ch-4 sp, *ch1, dc4 in ch-4 sp; rep from * to last ch-4 sp, dc2 in ch-4 sp, dc2tog in ch-4 sp, dc in last sc. 2 sts dec.

Row 3: Ch1, sc in first dc, ch3, sc in ch-1 sp, *ch4, sc in ch-1 sp; rep from * to end, ending with ch 3, sc in 3rd ch of beginning ch-3.

Row 4 (Dec row): Ch3, dc2tog in ch-3 sp, dc2 in same ch-3 sp, *ch1, dc4 in ch-4 sp; rep from * to last ch-3 sp, dc in ch-3 sp, dc2tog in ch-3 sp, dc in last sc. 2 sts dec.

Row 5: Ch1, sc in first dc, ch2, sc in ch-1 sp, *ch4, sc in ch-1 sp; rep from * to end, ending with ch 2, sc in 3rd ch of beginning ch-3.

Continue in this manner, decreasing 1 st at beginning and end of every RS row 2 (5, 8, 5, 7) more times. 62 (66, 70, 76, 82) sts.

Work even in patt until armhole measures 71/2 (8, 81/2, 9, 91/2)"/19 (20.5, 21.5, 23, 24) cm, ending with a WS row.

Shape Back Neck

Next row (RS): Ch3, work next 12 (13, 13, 15, 17) sts in patt, ending with dc.

Fasten off.

Sk center 38 (40, 44, 46, 48 sts), rejoin yarn. Ch3, work in patt to end.

Fasten off.

Front

Work same as for Back until piece measures 15"/38 cm, ending with a RS row.

Mark center ch-1 sp.

Right Front

Next row (WS): Work in patt to marked ch-1 sp, sc in marked sp, turn.

Continue in patt over these 45 (50, 55, 60, 65) sts until same length as back to armhole, ending with a RS row.

Shape Armhole

Next row (WS): Ch1, sl st in each st to 3rd (3rd, 3rd, 4th, 4th) ch-1 sp, sc in ch-1 sp, work in patt to end.

Shape armhole same as for back, decreasing at end of RS rows. 31 (33, 35, 38, 41) sts rem.

Work even until armhole measures 51/2 (6, 61/2, 7, 71/2)"/14 (15, 16.5, 17.5, 19) cm, ending with a RS row.

Shape Neck

Next row (WS): Work 12 (13, 13, 15, 17) sts in patt, ending with sc, turn.

Continue in patt over these sts until same length as back to shoulder. Fasten off.

Left Front

With WS facing, rejoin yarn in center ch-1 sp.

Next row (WS): Ch5 (counts as sc1, ch4), sc in ch-1 sp, continue in patt to end.

Continue in patt over these 45 (50, 55, 60, 65) sts until same length as back to armhole, ending with a RS row.

Shape Armhole

Next row (WS): Work in patt until 3 (3, 3, 4, 4) ch-1 sps remain, sc in 3rd (3rd, 3rd, 4th, 4th) ch-1 sp from end, turn.

Shape armhole same as for back, decreasing at beginning of RS rows. 31 (33, 35, 38, 41) sts rem.

Work even until armhole measures 51/2 (6, 61/2, 7, 71/2)"/14 (15, 16.5, 17.5, 19) cm, ending with a RS row.

Shape Neck

Next row (WS): Ch1, sl st over first 19 (20, 22, 23, 24) sts, ch1, work in patt to end.

Continue in patt over these sts until same length as back to shoulder. Fasten off.

Finishing

Sew side seams. Sew shoulder seams.

Neck Edging

Mark position of 8 button loops evenly spaced along right edge of front slit.

Join yarn at right shoulder seam. Work 1 rnd sc around neck edge, working 3 sc in each corner of front neck and sc2tog at bottom of front slit. At each marked button loop position, ch4 for button loop. Fasten off.

Armhole Edging

Join yarn at side seam. Work 1 rnd sc around armhole edge. Fasten off.

Sew buttons to left edge of front slit to correspond with buttonholes. Weave in ends. Block.

Montgomery

This button-front tank works well both layered and on its own. The shaped waist and bands of open stitchwork flatter just about any figure.

SKILL LEVEL
Intermediate

SIZES
Women's Extra Small (Small, Medium, Large, Extra Large)

FINISHED MEASUREMENTS
Bust: 33 (36¾, 40½, 44¼, 48)"/84 (93.5, 103, 112.5, 122) cm

YARN
Fibra Natura Flax, light weight #3 yarn (100% linen; 137 yd./1.75 oz., 125 m/50 g per skein)
- 5 (5, 6, 6, 7) skeins #101 Buttercream

HOOKS & NOTIONS
- US size G-6/4.25 mm crochet hook
- Locking stitch markers
- Tapestry needle
- 9 buttons, ⅝"/15 mm diameter

GAUGE
17 sts and 14 rows in Alternating Stripe patt = 4"/10 cm
17 sts and 10 rows in V-stitch patt = 4"/10 cm

PATTERN NOTE
- Turning chain is not included in stitch counts.

STITCH PATTERNS

Alternating Stripe Pattern
Row 1 (WS): Ch1, sc in each st to end.
Row 2 (RS): Ch3, dc in each st to end.
Rep Rows 1–2 for patt.

V-Stitch Pattern

Rows 1, 3, and 5 (RS): Ch3, *dc in first st, sk 1, dc3 in next st, sk 1; rep from * to last st, dc in last st.

Rows 2 and 4 (WS): Ch3, dc2 in first st, *sk 1, dc in next st, sk 1, dc3 in next st; rep from * to last 4 sts, sk 1, dc in next st, sk 1, dc2 in last st.

Body

Ch 138 (154, 170, 186, 202).

Row 1 (RS): Sc in 2nd ch from hook and in each ch to end. 137 (153, 169, 185, 201) sts.

Rows 2–4: Ch 1, sc in each st to end.

Work 5 rows of V-Stitch patt.

Begin working Alternating Stripe patt. Work even until piece measures 4"/10 cm, ending with a WS row.

Shape Waist

Place shaping markers on each side of center 35 (39, 43, 47, 51) sts and 17 (19, 21, 23, 25) sts away from each end. 4 markers total.

Next row (Dec row) (RS): Work in patt to first marker, dc2tog, work in patt to 2 sts before second marker, dc2tog, work in patt to third marker, dc2tog, work in patt to 2 sts before last marker, dc2tog, work in patt to end. 4 sts dec. Move markers up to current row as you work.

Rep Dec row every RS row 3 more times.

Work 1 WS row even in Alternating Stripe patt.

Work 5 rows of V-Stitch patt.

Work Row 1 of Alternating Stripe patt.

Check placement of markers on each side of center 35 (39, 43, 47, 51) sts, and 17 (19, 21, 23, 25) sts away from each end. 4 markers total.

Work remainder of piece in Alternating Stripe patt.

Next row (Inc row) (RS): Work in patt to first marker, dc2 in next st, work in patt to 1 st before second marker, dc2 in next st, work in patt to third marker, dc2 in next st, work in patt to 1 st before last marker, dc2 in next st, work in patt to end. 4 sts inc. Move markers up to current row as you work.

Rep Inc row every RS row 3 more times. 137 (153, 169, 185, 201) sts.

Work even in patt until piece measures 15"/38 cm, ending with a WS row.

Divide for Armholes

Next row (RS): Ch3, dc in next 28 (31, 34, 37, 40) sts, hdc in next st, sc in next st, sl st in next 8 (10, 12, 14, 16) sts, sc in next st, hdc in next st, dc in next 57 (63, 69, 75, 81) sts, hdc in next st, sc in next st, sl st in next 8 (10, 12, 14, 16) sts, sc in next st, hdc in next st, dc in next st and in each st to end.

Continue on 28 (31, 34, 37, 40) left front dcs only.

Left Front

Row 1 (WS): Ch1, sc in each st to end.

Shape Armhole and Front Neck

Row 2 (RS): Sl st in first 4 (5, 6, 7, 8) sts, ch3, dc2tog, dc in next 20 (22, 24, 26, 28) sts, dc2tog, turn work. 22 (24, 26, 28, 30) sts.

Row 3: Ch1, sc in each st to end.

Row 4 (Dec row): Ch3, dc2tog, dc to last 2 sts, dc2tog. 2 sts dec.

Rep Dec row every RS row 3 (4, 5, 5, 6) more times. 14 (14, 14, 16, 16) sts.

Next row (Neck Edge Dec row) (RS): Ch3, dc in each st to last 2 sts, dc2tog. 1 st dec.

Rep Neck Edge Dec row every RS row 2 (1, 0, 1, 0) more times. 11 (12, 13, 14, 15) sts.

Work even in Alternating Stripe patt until armhole measures 6½ (7, 7½, 8, 8½)"/16.5 (18, 19, 20.5, 21.5) cm, ending with a WS row.

Fasten off.

Right Front

Rejoin yarn to right front sts at armhole edge, starting with last dc before hdc.

Row 1 (WS): Ch1, sc in each st to end. 28 (31, 34, 37, 40) sts.

Shape Armhole and Front Neck

Row 2 (RS): Sl st in first 4 (5, 6, 7, 8) sts, ch3, dc2tog, dc to last 2 sts, dc2tog. 22 (24, 26, 28, 30) sts.

Row 3: Ch1, sc in each st to end.

Row 4 (Dec row): Ch3, dc2tog, dc to last 2 sts, dc2tog. 2 sts dec.

Rep Dec row every RS row 3 (4, 5, 5, 6) more times. 14 (14, 14, 16, 16) sts.

Next row (Neck Edge Dec row) (RS): Ch3, dc2tog, dc in each st to end. 1 st dec.

Rep Neck Edge Dec row every RS row 2 (1, 0, 1, 0) more times. 11 (12, 13, 14, 15) sts.

Work even in Alternating Stripe patt until armhole measures 6½ (7, 7½, 8, 8½)"/16.5 (18, 19, 20.5, 21.5) cm, ending with a WS row.

Fasten off.

Back

Rejoin yarn to back sts at left armhole edge, starting with last dc before hdc.

Row 1 (WS): Ch1, sc in each dc. 57 (63, 69, 75, 81) sts.

Row 2 (Dec row) (RS): Ch3, dc2tog, dc to last 2 sts, dc2tog. 2 sts dec.

Rep Dec row every RS row 4 (5, 6, 6, 7) more times. 47 (51, 55, 61, 65) sts.

Work even until armhole measures 6 (6½, 7, 7½, 8)"/15 (16.5, 18, 19, 20.5) cm, ending with a WS row.

Next row (RS): Ch3, dc 10 (11, 12, 13, 14), dc2tog, turn work.

Next row (WS): Ch1, sc in each st to end.

Fasten off.

Sk 23 (25, 27, 31, 33) sts at center neck and rejoin yarn for left back shoulder.

Next row (RS): Ch3, dc in each st to last 2 sts, dc2tog. 11 (12, 13, 14, 15) sts.

Next row (WS): Ch1, sc in each st to end. Fasten off.

Finishing

Sew shoulder seams.

Armhole Edging

Join yarn at side seam. Work 1 rnd sc around armhole edge. Fasten off.

Front and Neck Edging

Join yarn at lower right front corner.

Row 1 (RS): Sc up right front edge to beginning of neck shaping, sc3 in corner, sc around neck edge to left front neck corner, sc3 in corner, sc down left front edge to lower corner, turn work.

Row 2 (Buttonhole row) (WS): Sc in each sc to left neck corner, sc3 in corner st, sc around left neck edge, sc2tog at beginning of back neck, sc in each sc to end of back neck, sc2tog, sc around right neck edge to corner, sc3 in corner st, sc in next st, *ch2, sk2, sc in next 6 sts; rep from * 7 more times, ch2, sk2, sc in each st to end.

Row 3: Sc in each sc and sc 2 in each ch-2 sp to corner, sc3 in corner st, sc around neck edge to left neck corner, sc3 in corner st, sc in each sc to end.

Row 4: Sc in each sc to left neck corner, sc3 in corner st, sc around left neck edge, sc2tog at beginning of back neck, sc in each sc to end of back neck, sc2tog, sc around right neck edge to corner, sc3 in corner st, sc in each sc to end.

Fasten off.

Sew buttons to left front to correspond with buttonholes.

Weave in ends. Block lightly.

Valencia

Here is a classic that belongs in every wardrobe. The scoop neck, waist shaping, and scalloped edging elevate this tank beyond the basic. You'll want to live in it all summer long.

SKILL LEVEL
Easy

SIZES
Women's Extra Small (Small, Medium, Large, Extra Large, 2X Large)

FINISHED MEASUREMENTS
Bust: 29¼ (33½, 37¾, 42¼, 46½, 50¾)"/74.5 (85, 96, 107, 118, 128.5) cm

YARN
Universal Yarn Cotton Supreme DK, light weight #3 yarn (100% cotton; 230 yd./3.5 oz., 210 m/100 g per skein)
- 2 (3, 3, 4, 4, 4) skeins #702 Ecru

HOOKS & NOTIONS
- US size H-8/5 mm crochet hook
- Tapestry needle

GAUGE
15 sts and 11 rows in hdc = 4"/10 cm

PATTERN NOTE
- Turning chain is not included in stitch counts.

Back

Ch 59 (67, 75, 83, 91, 99).
Row 1 (RS): Hdc in 3rd ch from hook and in each ch to end. 57 (65, 73, 81, 89, 97) hdc.
Row 2: Ch2 (does not count as a st), hdc in each st to end. Rep Row 2 for patt.
Work even until piece measures 2"/5 cm, ending with a WS row.

Shape Waist

Next row (Dec row) (RS): Ch2, hdc2tog over first 2 sts, hdc to last 2 sts, hdc2tog. 2 sts dec.

Rep Dec row every RS row 3 more times. 49 (57, 65, 73, 81, 89) sts.

Work even until piece measures 7"/18 cm, ending with a WS row.

Next row (Inc row) (RS): Ch2, 2 hdc in first st, hdc to last st, 2 hdc in last st. 2 sts inc.

Rep Inc row every RS row 3 more times. 57 (65, 73, 81, 89, 97) sts.

Work even until piece measures 13"/33 cm, ending with a WS row, and ending last row 3 (4, 5, 6, 7, 8) sts before end.

Shape Armholes

Row 1 (RS): Ch2, hdc in each st to last 3 (4, 5, 6, 7, 8) sts.

Row 2 (Dec row) (WS): Ch2, hdc2tog over first 2 sts, hdc to last 2 sts, hdc2tog. 2 sts dec.

Rep Dec row every row 3 (5, 7, 9, 11, 13) more times. 43 (45, 47, 49, 51, 53) sts.

Work even until armholes measure 4 (4½, 5, 5½, 6, 6½)"/10 (11.5, 12.5, 14, 15, 16.5) cm, ending with a WS row.

Shape Back Neck

Row 1 (RS): Ch2, hdc in next 10 (11, 11, 12, 13, 14) sts, hdc2tog over next 2 sts. Continue on these 11 (12, 12, 13, 14, 15) sts only for right back shoulder.

Row 2 (WS): Ch2, hdc2tog over first 2 sts, hdc to end.

Row 3: Ch2, hdc in each st to last 2 sts, hdc2tog.

Row 4: Ch2, hdc2tog over first 2 sts, hdc to end. 8 (9, 9, 10, 11, 12) sts.

Row 5: Ch2, hdc to end. Fasten off.

Left Back Shoulder

Sk 19 (19, 21, 21, 21, 21) sts at center neck and rejoin yarn for left back shoulder.

Row 1 (RS): Ch2, hdc2tog over first 2 sts, hdc to end. 11 (12, 12, 13, 14, 15) sts.

Row 2 (WS): Ch2, hdc in each st to last 2 sts, hdc2tog.

Row 3: Ch2, hdc2tog over first 2 sts, hdc to end.

Row 4: Ch2, hdc in each st to last 2 sts, hdc2tog. 8 (9, 9, 10, 11, 12) sts.

Row 5: Ch2, hdc to end. Fasten off.

Front

Work same as for Back until armhole measures 2 (2½, 3, 3, 3½, 3½)"/5 (6.5, 7.5, 7.5, 9, 9) cm, ending with a WS row.

NOTE: For sizes Medium, Large, Extra Large, and 2X Large, front neck shaping begins before armhole shaping is complete.

Shape Front Neck

Mark center 15 (15, 17, 17, 17, 17) sts. Continue armhole shaping, if necessary, while working neck shaping.

Row 1 (RS): Work in patt to 2 sts before marked sts, hdc2tog. 1 st dec at neck edge. Continue on these sts only for left front shoulder.

Row 2 (WS): Ch2, hdc2tog over first 2 sts, work in patt to end. 1 st dec at neck edge.

Rep these 2 rows 2 more times. 6 sts dec at neck edge total.

When armhole and neck shaping is complete, 8 (9, 9, 10, 11, 12) sts remain.

Work even until same length as back. Fasten off.

Right Front Shoulder

Sk 15 (15, 17, 17, 17, 17) marked sts at center neck and rejoin yarn for right front shoulder.

Row 1 (RS): Ch2, hdc2tog over first 2 sts, work in patt to end, continuing armhole shaping if necessary. 1 st dec at neck edge.

Row 2 (WS): Work in patt to last 2 sts, hdc2tog. 1 st dec at neck edge.

Rep these 2 rows 2 more times. 6 sts dec at neck edge total.

When armhole and neck shaping is complete, 8 (9, 9, 10, 11, 12) sts remain.
Work even until same length as back. Fasten off.

Finishing

Sew side seams. Sew shoulder seams.

Neck Edging

Join yarn at right shoulder seam. Work 1 rnd sc around neck edge. Count sts and adjust if necessary to make the total a multiple of 4 sts.

Next rnd: *Sk 1, 5 hdc in next st, sk 1, sl st in next st; rep from * to end of rnd. Fasten off.

Armhole Edging

Join yarn at side seam. Work 1 rnd sc around armhole edge. Count sts and adjust if necessary to make the total a multiple of 4 sts.

Next rnd: *Sk 1, 5 hdc in next st, sk 1, sl st in next st; rep from * to end of rnd.

Fasten off.

Hem Edging

Join yarn at side seam. Work 1 rnd sc around hem edge. Count sts and adjust if necessary to make the total a multiple of 4 sts.

Next rnd: *Sk 1, 5 hdc in next st, sk 1, sl st in next st; rep from * to end of rnd.

Fasten off.

Weave in ends. Block lightly.

Divisidero

The curved hem and A-line shape of this tank let you cover your behind without being all covered up. The beautiful linen yarn and deep scoop neck keep it cool.

SKILL LEVEL
Easy

SIZES
Women's Extra Small (Small, Medium, Large, Extra Large, 2X Large)

FINISHED MEASUREMENTS
Bust: 32 (35¾, 39½, 43, 46¾, 50½)"/81.5 (91, 100.5, 109, 118.5, 128.5) cm

YARN
Quince & Co. Kestrel, medium weight #4 yarn (100% organic linen; 76 yd./1.75 oz., 70 m/50 g per skein)
- 6 (7, 7, 8, 9, 10) skeins #502 Porpoise

HOOKS & NOTIONS
- US size J-10/6 mm crochet hook
- Tapestry needle

GAUGE
13 sts and 10 rows in hdc = 4"/10 cm

PATTERN NOTES
- Divisidero is worked in one piece. The curved lower edge is shaped with short rows.
- While it is worked in the round, the work is turned at the end of each round, so you will work both RS and WS rounds.

- Turning ch counts as hdc throughout.

Back

Ch 130 (142, 154, 166, 178, 190).

Rnd 1 (RS): Hdc in 3rd ch from hook and in each ch to end, join with sl st in top of ch, turn. 128 (140, 152, 164, 176, 188) hdc.

Rnd 2 (WS): Ch2 (counts as hdc), hdc in each st to end, join with sl st in beginning ch-2, turn.

Short row 1 (RS): Ch2, hdc 24 (30, 36, 42, 48, 54), turn.

Short row 2 (WS): Ch2, hdc in each hdc, hdc2tog over beginning ch-2 of prior row and next st in Rnd 2 below, hdc in next 6 hdc, turn.

Short row 3: Ch2, hdc in each hdc, hdc2tog over beginning ch-2 of prior row and next st in Rnd 2 below, hdc in next 6 hdc turn.

Short rows 4–13: Rep Short Rows 2 and 3 five more times.

Short row 14 (WS): Ch2, hdc in each hdc, hdc2tog over beginning ch-2 of prior row and next st of Rnd 2 below, hdc in next 6 hdc, turn.

Rnd 3 (RS): Ch2, hdc in each hdc, hdc2tog over beginning ch-2 of prior row and next st of Rnd 2 below, hdc to end of rnd, join with sl st in beginning ch-2. 114 (126, 138, 150, 162, 174) hdc. Break yarn.

Sk next 16 sts and rejoin yarn with WS facing. This is right "side seam."

Rnd 4: Ch2, hdc in each hdc, join with sl st in beginning ch-2, turn.

Rnds 5–6: Rep Rnd 4 twice.

Rnd 7: Ch2, hdc 3, hdc2tog over next 2 hdc, hdc 47 (53, 59, 65, 71, 77), hdc2tog over next 2 hdc, hdc6, hdc2tog over next 2 hdc, hdc to last 5 hdc, hdc2tog over next 2 hdc, hdc3, join with sl st in beginning ch-2, turn. 110 (122, 134, 146, 158, 170) hdc.

Rnds 8–12: Rep Rnd 4 five times.

Rnd 13: Ch2, hdc 3, hdc2tog over next 2 hdc, hdc 45 (51, 57, 63, 69, 75), hdc2tog over next 2 hdc, hdc6, hdc2tog over next 2 hdc, hdc to last 5 hdc, hdc2tog over next 2 hdc, hdc3, join with sl st in beginning ch-2, turn. 106 (118, 130, 142, 154, 166) hdc.

Rnds 14–18: Rep Rnd 4 five times.

Rnd 19: Ch2, hdc2tog over first 2 hdc, hdc 51 (57, 63, 69, 75, 81), hdc2tog over next 2 hdc, hdc to end, join with sl st in beginning ch-2, turn. 104 (116, 128, 140, 152, 164) hdc.

Rep [Rnd 4] 1 (1, 3, 3, 5, 5) more times. Fasten off.

Shape Armholes

With RS facing, counting from end of rnd, sk 3 (4, 5, 6, 7, 8) hdc and join yarn.

Row 1 (RS): Ch2, hdc 46 (50, 54, 58, 62, 66), turn.

Row 2 (WS): Ch2, hdc2tog, hdc to last hdc, hdc2tog, hdc in top of beginning ch-2, turn. 2 sts dec.

Rep [Row 2] 4 (5, 6, 8, 9, 10) more times. 36 (38, 40, 40, 42, 44) hdc.

Work 8 (7, 8, 6, 7, 6) rows even in hdc.

Shape Back Neck

Row 1 (RS): Ch2, hdc 6, hdc2tog, turn.

Row 2 (WS): Ch2, hdc2tog, hdc to end, turn.

Work 4 rows even in hdc. Fasten off.

With RS facing, sk 20 (22, 24, 24, 26, 28) hdc and rejoin yarn.

Next row (RS): Ch2, hdc2tog, hdc to end, turn.

Next row (WS): Ch2, hdc 5, hdctog, turn.

Work 4 rows even in hdc. Fasten off.

Front

With RS facing, sk 6 (8, 10, 12, 14, 16) sts for armhole and join yarn.

Row 1 (RS): Ch2, hdc 46 (50, 54, 58, 62, 66), turn.

Row 2 (WS): Ch2, hdc2tog, hdc to last hdc, hdc2tog, hdc in top of beginning ch-2, turn. 2 sts dec.

Rep [Row 2] 2 more times. 40 (44, 48, 52, 56, 60) hdc.

Shape Front Neck

Row 1 (RS): Ch2, hdc2tog, hdc 6 (7, 8, 10, 11, 12), hdc2tog, turn.

Row 2 (WS): Ch2, hdc2tog, hdc to last 2 hdc, hdc2tog, turn.

Continue dec at armhole edge only every row 0 (1, 2, 4, 5, 6) more time(s). 8 sts rem.

Work 14 (13, 14, 12, 13, 12) rows even in hdc. Fasten off.

With RS facing, sk 20 (22, 24, 24, 26, 28) hdc at center front neck and join yarn.

Next row (RS): Ch2, hdc2tog, hdc to last 2 hdc, hdc2tog, turn.

Next row (WS): Ch2, hdc2tog, hdc to last 2 hdc, hdc2tog, turn.

Continue dec at armhole edge only every row 0 (1, 2, 4, 5, 6) more time(s). 8 sts rem.

Work 14 (13, 14, 12, 13, 12) rows even in hdc. Fasten off.

Finishing

Sew shoulder seams.

Neck Edging

Join yarn at right shoulder seam. Work 1 rnd sc around neck edge.

Armhole Edging

Join yarn at side seam. Work 1 rnd sc around armhole edge. Weave in ends. Block lightly.

Folsom

Is there any silhouette more flattering than a wrap? With its deep V-neck and built-in waist definition, this feminine top will pair well with tailored skirts and pants.

SKILL LEVEL
Intermediate

SIZES
Women's Extra Small (Small, Medium, Large, Extra Large, 2X Large)

FINISHED MEASUREMENTS
Bust: 32 (36½, 40, 44½, 48, 52½)"/81.5 (93, 101.5, 113, 122, 133.5) cm

YARN
Patons Silk Bamboo, light weight #3 yarn (70% viscose from bamboo, 30% silk; 102 yd./2.2 oz., 93 m/65 g per skein)
- 6 (7, 8, 9, 10, 11) skeins #85219 Sea

HOOKS & NOTIONS
- US size H-8/5 mm crochet hook
- Removable stitch markers or safety pins
- Tapestry needle

GAUGE
14 sts and 11 rows in Brick Stitch patt = 4"/10 cm

PATTERN NOTES
- Folsom is worked in one piece from the bottom up. The only seams are at the shoulders.
- The stitch count in this pattern changes from row to row. Count stitches at the end of RS double crochet rows only.
- Turning chain is not counted as a stitch.

STITCH PATTERN

Brick Stitch Pattern
Row 1 (WS): Ch1, sc in first dc, ch2, sk next dc, sc in sp between last skipped st and next dc, *ch2, sk next 2 dc, sc in sp between

last skipped st and next dc; rep from * to end, ending with sc in 3rd ch of beginning ch-3.

Row 2 (RS): Ch3, 2 dc in each ch-2 sp to last ch-2 sp, dc in last ch-2 sp, dc in last sc.

Rep Rows 1–2 for patt.

Back and Right Front

Ch 169 (189, 211, 231, 253, 273).

Row 1 (RS): Dc in 4th ch from hook, dc in each ch to end. 166 (186, 208, 228, 250, 270) dc.

Work 5 rows in Brick St patt.

Next row (RS): Ch3, [2 dc in ch-2 sp] 26 times, place marker, [2 dc in ch-2 sp] 31 times, place marker, 2 dc in each ch-2 sp to end.

Next row (WS): Work Row 1 of Brick St patt.

Next row (Dec row): *Work in patt to ch-2 sp before marker, 1 dc in next 2 ch-2 sps, moving marker to between these 2 dc; rep from * once, work in patt to end. 4 sts dec.

Continuing in patt, rep Dec row every RS row 7 more times. 134 (154, 176, 196, 218, 238) dc.

Work Row 1 of Brick St patt.

Shape Front Wrap

Row 1 (RS): Ch3, dc2tog in first 2 ch-2 sps, *work in patt to ch-2 sp before marker, dc3 in next ch-2 sp twice, moving marker to between these two 3-dc groups; rep from * once, work in patt to last 2 ch-2 sps, dc2tog in last 2 ch-2 sps.

Row 2 (WS): Work Row 1 of Brick St patt.

Row 3: Ch3, dc2tog in first 2 ch-2 sps, work in patt to last 2 ch-2 sps, dc2tog in last 2 ch-2 sps. 4 sts dec.

Row 4: Rep Row 2.

Rep [Rows 1–4] 4 more times. 114 (134, 156, 176, 198, 218) dc.

Shape Right Front Neck and Armhole

Row 1 (RS): Ch3, dc2tog in first 2 ch-2 sps, [2 dc in ch-2 sp] 11 (13, 17, 20, 23, 26) times, dc2tog in next 2 ch-2 sps, turn. 26 (30, 38, 44, 50, 56) dc.

Row 2: Work Row 1 of Brick St patt.

Rep [Rows 1–2] 1 (2, 3, 4, 5, 6) more times. 18 (18, 22, 24, 26, 28) dc.

Next row (RS): Ch3, dc2tog in first 2 ch-2 sps, work in patt to end.

Next row: Work Row 1 of Brick St patt.

Rep last 2 rows 5 (5, 7, 7, 8, 9) more times. 6 (6, 6, 8, 8, 8) dc.

Work 4 (2, 0, 0, 0, 0) rows even in Brick St patt.

Fasten off.

Back and Left Front

With RS facing, sk 3 (4, 5, 5, 6, 7) ch-2 sps for armhole and rejoin yarn.

Row 1 (RS): Ch3, dc2tog in first 2 ch-2 sps, [2 dc in ch-2 sp] 21 (24, 26, 30, 32, 35) times, dc2tog in next 2 ch-2 sps, turn. 46 (52, 56, 64, 68, 74) dc.

Row 2 (WS): Work Row 1 of Brick St patt.

Rep [Rows 1–2] 1 (2, 3, 4, 5, 6) more times. 42 (44, 44, 48, 48, 50) dc.

Work even until same length as right front to shoulder, ending with a WS row.

Fasten off.

Shape Left Front Neck and Armhole

With RS facing, sk 3 (4, 5, 5, 6, 7) ch-2 sps for armhole and rejoin yarn.

Row 1 (RS): Ch3, dc2tog in first 2 ch-2 sps, 2 dc in each ch-2 sp to last 2 ch-2 sps, dc2tog in next 2 ch-2 sps, turn. 26 (30, 38, 44, 50, 56) dc.

Row 2: Work Row 1 of Brick St patt.

Rep [Rows 1–2] 1 (2, 3, 4, 5, 6) more times. 18 (18, 22, 24, 26, 28) dc.

Next row (RS): Ch3, 2 dc in each ch-2 sp to last 2 ch-2 sps, dc2tog in next 2 ch-2 sps.

Next row: Work Row 1 of Brick St patt.

Rep last 2 rows 5 (5, 7, 7, 8, 9) more times. 6 (6, 6, 8, 8, 8) dc.

Work 4 (2, 0, 0, 0, 0) rows even in patt.

Fasten off.

Finishing

Sew shoulder seams.

Ties

Join yarn at beginning of right front wrap shaping. Ch 40 (45, 50, 55, 60, 65). Fasten off.

Join yarn at beginning of left front wrap shaping. Ch 110 (120, 130, 140, 150, 160). Fasten off.

Front and Neck Edging

Join yarn at lower right front corner. Sc evenly along front edge to tie, sc in each st of ch, sc3 in end of ch, sc along other side of ch, sc around neck edge to tie at left front, sc in each st of ch, sc3 in end of ch, sc along other side of ch, sc down left front to lower edge. Fasten off.

Armhole Edging

Join yarn at center of underarm and work 1 rnd of sc around armhole edge. Fasten off.

Weave in ends. Block.

Pacific

The vertical waves in this openwork stitch pattern remind me of kelp swaying with the motion of the sea. The hand-dyed silk yarn makes this piece a luxury you'll love to wear.

SKILL LEVEL
Easy

SIZES
Women's Extra Small (Small, Medium, Large, Extra Large)

FINISHED MEASUREMENTS
Bust: 34¾ (38¼, 41¾, 45¼, 49)"/88.5 (97, 106, 115, 124.5) cm

YARN
LB Collection One Hundred Percent Silk, fine weight #2 yarn (100% silk; 163 yd./1.75 oz., 150 m/50 g per skein)
* 3 (3, 4, 4, 5) skeins #201 Gemini

HOOKS & NOTIONS
* US size H-8/5 mm crochet hook
* Tapestry needle

GAUGE
18 sts and 9 rows in hdc = 4"/10 cm

PATTERN NOTE
* Turning chain is included in stitch counts throughout.

STITCH PATTERN

Sliding Blocks Pattern

Row 1 (RS): Ch3, sk first dc, *dc in next 5 dc, ch3, sk next 3 dc; rep from * to end, ending with dc in last 3 dc, dc in 3rd ch of beginning ch-3.

Row 2 (WS): Ch3, sk first dc, dc in next 3 dc, *dc in ch-3 sp, ch3, sk next dc, dc in next 4 dc; rep from * to end, end with dc in 3rd ch of beginning ch-3.

Row 3: Ch3, sk first dc, dc in next 3 dc, *sk next dc, ch3, dc in ch-3 sp, dc in next 4 dc; rep from * to end, ending with dc in 3rd ch of beginning ch-3.

Row 4: Ch4, sk first 2 dc, *dc in next 4 dc, dc in ch-3 sp, ch3, sk next dc; rep from * to end, ending with dc in last 2 dc, dc in 3rd ch of beginning ch-3.

Row 5: Ch3, sk first dc, dc in next dc, *sk next dc, ch3, dc in ch-3 sp, dc in next 4 dc; rep from * to end, ending with sk next dc, ch2, dc in 3rd ch of beginning ch-4.

Row 6: Ch4, sk first 2 dc, dc in ch-2 sp, *dc in next 4 dc, sk next dc, ch3, dc in ch-3 sp; rep from * to end, ending dc in last dc, dc in 3rd ch of beginning ch-3.

Row 7: Ch3, sk first dc, dc in next 2 dc, *dc in ch-3 sp, ch3, sk next dc, dc in next 4 dc; rep from * to end, ending with dc in ch-4 sp, dc in 3rd ch of beginning ch-4.

Row 8: Ch3, sk first dc, *dc in next 4 dc, sk next dc, ch3, dc in ch-3 sp; rep from * to end, ending with dc in next 3 dc, dc in 3rd ch of beginning ch-3.

Row 9: Ch3, sk first dc, *dc in next 4 sts, dc in ch-3 sp, ch3, sk next dc; rep from * to end, ending with dc in last 3 dc, dc in 3rd ch of beginning ch-3.

Rep Rows 2–9 for patt.

Back

Ch 81 (89, 97, 105, 113).

Foundation row (WS): Dc in 4th ch from hook and in each ch to end. 78 (86, 94, 102, 110) sts.

Begin working Sliding Blocks patt.

Work even in patt until piece measures 13 (13, 13½, 14, 14½)"/3 (33, 34.5, 35.5, 37) cm, ending with a WS row.

Shape Armholes

Row 1 (RS): Ch1, sl st over next 3 (5, 7, 9, 11) sts, ch3, work in patt to last 3 (5, 7, 9, 11) sts, ending with dc, turn.

Row 2 (Dec row): Ch3, sk first dc, dc2tog over next 2 sts, work in patt to last 2 dc, dc2tog, dc in 3rd ch of beginning ch-3. 2 sts dec.

Rep Dec row every row 1 (2, 3, 4, 6) more times. 68 (70, 72, 74, 74) sts.

Work even in patt until armhole measures 6½ (6½, 7, 7½, 8)"/16.5 (16.5, 18, 19, 20.5) cm, ending with a WS row.

Shape Back Neck

Next row (RS): Work in patt across first 12 (13, 14, 15, 15) sts, dc in next 2 sts. Fasten off.

Sk center 40 sts and rejoin yarn. Ch3, dc in next st, work in patt to end. Fasten off.

Front

Work same as for back until armholes measure 3"/7.5 cm, ending with a WS row.

Mark center 32 sts.

Left Front

Row 1 (RS): Work in patt to 3 sts before marked center sts, dc2tog, dc in next st, turn.

Row 2 (WS): Ch3, sk first dc, dc2tog, work in patt to end.

Rows 3–4: Rep Rows 1–2. 14 (15, 16, 17, 17) sts.

Work even until same length as back to shoulder. Fasten off.

Right Front

With RS facing, rejoin yarn at second marker.

Row 1 (RS): Ch3, sk first dc, dc2tog, work in patt to end.

Row 2 (WS): Work in patt to last 2 sts, dc2tog, dc in 3rd ch of beginning ch-3.

Rows 3–4: Rep Rows 1–2. 14 (15, 16, 17, 17) sts.

Work even until same length as back to shoulder. Fasten off.

Finishing

Sew side seams. Sew shoulder seams.

Neck Edging

Join yarn at right shoulder seam. Work 1 rnd dc around neck edge, working 3 dc in each ch-3 sp. Fasten off.

Armhole Edging

Join yarn at side seam. Work 1 rnd sc around armhole edge.
Fasten off.
Weave in ends. Block lightly.

Sutter

This is an elegant top that is all about the yarn. The simple shape comes alive with gradient color and subtle sparkle.

SKILL LEVEL
Easy

SIZES
Women's Extra Small (Small, Medium, Large, Extra Large)

FINISHED MEASUREMENTS
Bust: 31½ (36, 39½, 44, 47½)"/80 (91.5, 100, 112, 120.5) cm

YARN
Berroco Captiva Metallic, medium weight #4 yarn (45% cotton, 23% polyester, 19% acrylic, 12% rayon, 1% other; 98 yd./1.75 oz., 90 m/50 g per skein)
- 2 (2, 3, 3, 3) skeins #7542 Antique Copper (A)
- 2 (2, 2, 3, 3) skeins #7540 Mascarpone (C)

Berroco Captiva, medium weight #4 yarn (60% cotton, 23% polyester, 17% acrylic; 98 yd./1.75 oz., 90 m/50 g per skein)
- 2 (2, 2, 3, 3) skeins #5506 Bronze (B)
- 1 (1, 1, 2, 2) skeins #5501 Venetian Lace (D)

HOOKS & NOTIONS
- US size I-9/5.5 mm crochet hook
- Tapestry needle

GAUGE
14 sts and 13 rows in Hi-Lo patt = 4"/10 cm

PATTERN NOTE
- Turning chain is not included in stitch counts.

STITCH PATTERN

Hi-Lo Pattern
Row 1: Ch1, *sc in dc, dc in sc; rep from * to end.
Rep Row 1 for patt.

Back

With A, ch 57 (65, 71, 79, 85).

Set-up row (WS): Sc in 2nd ch from hook and in each ch to end. 56 (64, 70, 78, 84) sts.

Begin working Hi-Lo patt.

When piece measures 5 (5, 5½, 5½, 6)"/12.5 (12.5, 14, 14, 15) cm, change to B.

Continue in Hi-Lo patt.

When piece measures 10 (10, 11, 11, 12)"/25.5 (25.5, 28, 28, 30.5) cm, change to C.

Continue in Hi-Lo patt until piece measures 13½ (13, 14½, 14, 15½)"/34.5 (33, 37, 35.5, 39.5) cm, ending with a WS row and ending last row 3 (4, 5, 6, 6) sts before end.

Shape Armholes

NOTE: The color is changed before armhole shaping is complete. Please read ahead.

Row 1 (RS): Ch1, work in established Hi-Lo patt to last 3 (4, 5, 6, 6) sts, turn work.

Rows 2–3: Ch 1, work in established Hi-Lo patt to last 2 (2, 2, 3, 4) sts, turn work. 46 (52, 56, 60, 64) sts.

Row 4 (Dec row): Ch1, sc2tog, *sc in dc, dc in sc; rep from * to last 3 sts, sc2tog, dc. 2 sts dec.

Rep Dec row every row 6 (8, 9, 10, 11) more times. 32 (34, 36, 38, 40) sts.

AT THE SAME TIME, when piece measures 15 (15, 16½, 16½, 18)"/38 (38, 42, 42, 45.5) cm, change to D.

Work even in patt until armhole measures 4½ (5, 5½, 6, 6½)"/11.5 (12.5, 14, 15, 16.5) cm, ending with a WS row.

Shape Back Neck

Next row (RS): Work 6 sts in patt, turn work. Continue on these sts only for right back shoulder.

Work 7 more rows even in patt. Fasten off.

Sk 20 (22, 24, 26, 28) sts at center neck and rejoin yarn for left back shoulder.

Work over remaining 6 sts only.

Work 8 rows even in patt. Fasten off.

Front

Work same as for back until armhole measures 3 (3½, 4, 4½, 5)"/7.5 (9, 10, 11.5, 12.5) cm, ending with a WS row.

NOTE: For all sizes except Extra Large, front neck shaping begins before armhole shaping is complete. Please read ahead.

Shape Front Neck

Mark center 20 (22, 24, 26, 28) sts.

Next row (RS): Work in patt to marked sts, turn work. Continue on these sts only for left front shoulder.

Continuing armhole shaping if necessary, work in patt until same length as back to shoulder. When all armhole shaping is complete, 6 sts remain. Fasten off.

Sk 20 (22, 24, 26, 28) marked sts at center neck and rejoin yarn for right front shoulder.

Continuing armhole shaping if necessary, work in patt until same length as back to shoulder. When all armhole shaping is complete, 6 sts remain. Fasten off.

Finishing

Sew side seams. Sew shoulder seams.

Neck Edging

With D, join yarn at right shoulder seam. Work 1 rnd sc around neck edge. Fasten off.

Armhole Edging

With D, join yarn at side seam. Work 1 rnd sc around armhole edge. Fasten off.

Weave in ends. Block lightly.

Balboa

This tank has a twirly handkerchief hem and straps that cross in the back. The spatter dye on the linen-and-cotton blend yarn adds to the modern bohemian vibe.

SKILL LEVEL
Intermediate

SIZES
Women's Extra Small (Small, Medium, Large, Extra Large)

FINISHED MEASUREMENTS
Bust: 34¼ (37¾, 41, 44½, 48)"/87 (96, 104, 113, 122) cm

YARN
Fibra Natura Good Earth Adorn, medium weight #4 yarn (53% cotton, 47% linen; 204 yd./3.5 oz., 187 m/100 g per skein)
- 5 (6, 6, 7, 8) skeins #302 Adobe

HOOKS & NOTIONS
- US size H-8/5 mm crochet hook
- Tapestry needle

GAUGE
14 sts and 12 rows in hdc = 4"/10 cm

PATTERN NOTE
- This tank starts at the top of the bib and is worked down toward the hem.

Bib

Ch 34.

Row 1 (WS): Hdc in 3rd ch from hook and in each ch to end. 32 hdc.

Row 2 (RS): Ch2, turn, hdc in first hdc, sk 1, *hdc3 in next hdc, sk 2 hdc; rep from * to last 3 hdc, hdc3 in next hdc, sk 1 hdc, hdc2 in last hdc.

Row 3: Ch2, hdc in first hdc, hdc3 in each sp between groups of hdc to end, hdc in last hdc.

Row 4: Ch2, hdc3 in each sp between groups of hdc to end, hdc in last hdc.

Row 5: Ch2, hdc3 in each sp between groups of hdc to end, ending with hdc3 in 2nd ch of beginning ch-2.

Row 6: Ch2, hdc2 in first hdc, hdc3 in each sp between groups of hdc to end, ending with hdc2 in 2nd ch of beginning ch-2.

Row 7: Ch2, hdc2 in first hdc, hdc3 in each sp between groups of hdc to end, ending with hdc2 in 2nd ch of beginning ch-2.

Row 8: Ch2, hdc in first hdc, hdc3 in each sp between groups of hdc to end, ending with hdc in 2nd ch of beginning ch-2.

Row 9: Ch2, hdc3 in each sp between groups of hdc to end, ending with hdc in 2nd ch of beginning ch-2.

Row 10: Ch2, hdc3 in each sp between groups of hdc to end, ending with hdc in 2nd ch of beginning ch-2.

Row 11: Ch2, hdc2 in first hdc, hdc3 in each sp between groups of hdc to end, ending with hdc2 in 2nd ch of beginning ch-2.

Row 12: Ch2, hdc in first hdc, hdc3 in each sp between groups of hdc to end, ending with hdc2 in 2nd ch of beginning ch-2. 54 hdc. Do not turn at end of row.

Skirt

Ch 66 (78, 90, 102, 114), join with sl st to 2nd ch of beginning ch-2 of Row 12. 120 (132, 144, 156, 168) sts.

Rnd 1: Sl st to first sp between groups of hdc, ch2, hdc2 in same sp, hdc3 in each sp to end of bib, hdc3 in first ch, *sk 2 ch, hdc3 in next ch; rep from * until 2 ch rem, sk 2 ch, join with sl st to 2nd ch of beginning ch-2.

Rnds 2–12: Rep Rnd 1 eleven more times. Fasten off and break yarn.

Locate center back by folding the piece in half, matching the corners of the bib. Mark sp between groups of hdc at center back.

Rejoin yarn at marked sp.

Rnd 13: Ch2, hdc2 in same sp, hdc3 in next 2 (2, 3, 3, 4) sps between groups of hdc, [hdc2, ch1, hdc2] in next sp, hdc3 in next 5 (6, 6, 7, 7) sps between groups of hdc, [hdc2, ch1, hdc2] in next sp, hdc3 in next 5 (6, 6, 7, 7) sps between groups of hdc, [hdc2, ch1, hdc2] in next sp, hdcc3 in next 7 (7, 9, 9, 11) sps between groups of hdc, [hdc2, ch1, hdc2] in next sp, hdc3 in next 5 (6, 6, 7, 7) sps between groups of hdc, [hdc2, ch1, hdc2] in next sp, hdc3 in next 5 (6, 6, 7, 7) sps between groups of hdc, [hdc2, ch1, hdc2] in next sp, hdc3 in each sp between groups of hdc to end, join with sl st to 2nd ch of beginning ch-3.

Rnd 14: Ch2, hdc2 in same sp, *hdc3 in each sp between groups of hdc to ch-1 sp, [hdc2, ch1, hdc2] in ch-1 sp; rep from * 5 more times, hdc in each sp between groups of hdc to end, join with sl st to 2nd ch of beginning ch-3.

Rnds 15–30: Rep Rnd 14 sixteen more times.

Fasten off.

Finishing

Neck Edging

Work 1 rnd sc around upper edge of back and bib.

Straps

Ch 40. Join with sl st to upper corner of bib, ch1, sc in sl st and in each ch to end, sc3 in end of ch, working along other side of strap, sc in each ch to end.

Rep for second strap.

Mark attachment points for straps on back, 3"/7.5 cm on either side of center. Cross straps and sew in place, being careful not to twist straps.

Weave in ends. Block lightly.

27663209R00049